HEALING

FOR

HURTING PEOPLE

GOD'S ROAD MAP TO

WHOLENESS AND HAPPINESS

JESUS commanded Peter, His first pastor,
"*Feed* (care for) *My* (wounded and hurting) *Sheep*"
(John 21:16).

BY DR. JAMES WILKINS

DEDICATION

To my dear wife of seven years, whom I affectionately call my "Second Blessing." Among some of the dark waters which she has traveled through was the random shooting and murder of her baby boy on Mother's Day. Through sickness, accidents and disappointments she has maintained a sweet spirit, a love for the Lord and a ministering spirit to people.

In reference to her life-long nick name of Penny she often states, "I'm not worth a dollar or a dime, just one cent or a penny." Those who know her best all agree that she is real royalty and worth millions.

Healing Words for Hurting People is dedicated to a wonderful wife, friend, Christian, and mother, Grand-mother Lurene Margarett Wilkins.

FOREWORD

$\mathcal{K}$ ing David arose from the lowly status of a sheepherder to one of the most famous and successful men of all generations. *Healing Words for Hurting People* is based upon David's experience found in Psalm 116.

David's road to success started with an old-fashioned Holy Ghost conviction of sin, followed by an exuberance of joy unspeakable as he experienced the "new birth." For a period of time, he walked in the light of God's love and experienced the joys of being a new convert. **He was thrilled with life!** He was all but overcome daily with the excitement of knowing Christ and the blessings of God. His life couldn't have been sweeter; songs of praise poured forth from his lips.

Then It Happened! His light became **darkness**, his joy became **grief**, his praise became **bitterness,** as he experienced the heartbreak of **being offended and wounded** as a new Christian. This same experience, being hurt or offended, happens to every new believer. Job spoke of life as, *"few day, and full of trouble"* (Job 14:1).

Jesus, the night before He was crucified, warned His disciples of the severe offenses that they would encounter.

"These things have I spoken unto you, that ye should not be offended" (John 16:1).

DAVID EXPERIENCED IT ALL! He exclaimed, *"I was greatly afflicted."* He then expanded on his shock and dismay by proclaiming, *"All men are liars!"* **as he plunged into the depths of despair**.

This book is in obedience to the command Jesus made to His first pastor, *"Feed* (care for) *my* (wounded and hurting) *sheep"* (John 21:16). **As a pastor of 50 years, I have directed this book to the people who have been offended or who have become disenchanted with professed Christianity.**

What follows, is what Paul Harvey would describe as *"The Rest of the Story."* David begins his walk on the **"Road to Victory"** as a child of God. This road to victory and happiness could be stated as David's road back to wholeness. **It is a road well lit** and it is for all wounded hurting people. It is my prayer that many will find their healing through obeying the truths that David brought to light.

I humbly present this book and pray that God will use it to be a source of healing and help to you.

Prayerfully submitted,
Dr. James Wilkins

TABLE OF CONTENTS

"Daddy, can't you fix it?"

"It hurts so bad...!"

"Life is so unfair...!"

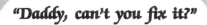

*H*ave you ever thought… There should be a manual that could repair a broken life?

"…there's a manual for the car, the television, the computer, and everything else in life – so it looks like there would be a manual, that would repair a broken heart, a broken dream, a broken life."

"There ought to be a book or a person who could help someone like me."

"I'd like to start again, but I don't know how…"

AT LAST! A MANUAL TO HELP REPAIR A BROKEN LIFE.

Chapter One

CHAPTER ONE

A COMMENTARY OF DAVID'S HEALING

PSALM 116:1-2

"I love the LORD, because he hath heard my voice and my supplications. Because he hath inclined his ear unto me, therefore will I call upon him as long as I live." As you read these verses, you can hear his heart **sing!** David is praising the Lord as he remembers the experience of salvation (recorded in verses 3 and 4).

PSALM 116:3

"The sorrows of death compassed me, and the pains of hell gat hold upon me: I found trouble and sorrow." In this verse, David describes the Holy Spirit's conviction, which all sinners must experience before true salvation. The Holy Spirit made him conscious that he was unprepared to die. The conviction grew as he realized the danger of hell and that he was going there. He found trouble and sorrow as he wrestled with his lost and hopeless condition.

PSALM 116:4

"Then called I upon the name of the LORD; O LORD, I beseech (beg) *thee, deliver my soul."* This hopeless,

lost condition caused David to call out to God and ask God to save him.

PSALM 116:5

"Gracious is the LORD, and righteous; yea, our God is merciful." No one has to wonder whether God answered David's prayer when they read of his exclamation of how gracious and merciful God is.

PSALM 116:6

"The LORD preserveth the simple: I was brought low, and he helped me." David exalts the Lord as he states that he was brought low and God helped him.

PSALM 116:7

"Return unto thy rest, O my soul; for the LORD hath dealt bountifully with thee." David speaks to himself saying that since the Lord has dealt bountifully with him, his soul has found peace and forgiveness. The horrible guilt and fear is gone.

PSALM 116:8

"For thou hast delivered my soul from death, mine eyes from tears, and my feet from falling." David exclaimed that he asked for mercy, but God gave him **deliverance** from death, **joy** instead of tears, and **security** instead of helplessness.

There is joy and victory coming from David's lips, which could be summarized by singing, "Oh, What a Savior!"

PSALM 116:9

"I will walk before the LORD in the land of the living." Here, David states his declaration of service to the Lord, as he walks in the land of the living (saved) with an absolute commitment to serve him.

PSALM 116:10

"I believed, therefore have I spoken: I was greatly afflicted." In the first part of this verse, David tells of the natural results of being saved. He started telling people of his salvation and declared his faith as he witnessed of God's greatness. When he began to witness and share his faith in his Savior, IT HAPPENED! **"I was greatly afflicted."**

PSALM 116:11
DAVID'S HEART-PIERCING SCREAM

"I said in my haste, All men are liars." When troubles began to compound and overwhelm his soul, it caused David to cry out in haste, *"I am greatly afflicted; **all men are liars, hypocrites!**"* In other words, David came to the place where he believed that everyone was a hypocrite and a liar. He felt deserted, which caused him to declare that there was not a real Christian in the whole land!

David plunged from the highest state of joy and happiness, to the lowest darkness of despair. He was overwhelmed! He was crushed.

THE SWEET SINGER

As one reflects on David's young life, he can see that he was a happy kid. He had the joy of the Lord in his soul and was the sweet singer of Israel. However, he had much, much more. In one day's time, he became

the NATIONAL HERO OF ISRAEL,
the PRIDE AND JOY of his mother and father,
he MARRIED THE KING'S DAUGHTER,
he became ROYALTY
and was EATING AT THE KING'S TABLE,
and he was GENERAL OF THE ARMY.

He was blessed on every side.

LIKE A BOLT OF LIGHTNING

THEN IT HAPPENED! The king of Israel (the king he loved, his own father-in-law) tried **to murder him!** Out of the blue, like a bolt of lightning, **he lost his wife, his position** and **became a hunted criminal.** His friends turned on him and he found that **he was on the run with a price on his head.** He was out in the wilderness all alone. He was tired and hungry – **greatly afflicted and greatly confused.**

PSALM 116:12

"What shall I render unto the LORD for all his benefits toward me?" David's heartbreak and wound caused him to have a great problem. How was he going to handle this offense and his future service to the Lord?

One can see David's reasoning as he questions what he should do. **David must have reasoned that it wasn't the Lord who let him down. No, God was the only one who helped him when he was lost and in despair. He probably reasoned that when he was lost and undone, full of conviction and fear, that it was God who heard his cry and saved him;** SO HE SHOULDN'T TAKE HIS ANGER OUT ON GOD, BECAUSE GOD WAS THE ONLY ONE WHO HELPED HIM.

PSALM 116:13

"I will take the cup of salvation, and call upon the name of the LORD." This verse reveals the answer to David's question of what he should do. In other words, David is saying that he will pray about it and that he will turn all of this horrible problem and hurt over to the Lord. This simple step of *"calling upon the name of the Lord"* was David's first step as he started on the **"Road to Victory!"**

PSALM 116:14

"I will pay my vows unto the LORD now in the presence of all his people." This verse reveals the decision David came to after turning his heartbreak over to the Lord. **In other words, he will keep his promise to the Lord. When he asked the Lord to save him from hell, he promised Him that he would serve Him.** Listen to David's declaration of God after praying about it. *"I will pay my vows unto the Lord now in the presence of all his people."* In other words, he would continue going to church regularly and serving God.

PSALM 116:15

"Precious in the sight of the LORD is the death of his saints." Here David declares a truth which is so profound, that few ever understand it. He is referring to the death of **his wants, his desires and his own will.** To die to self, means to come to the end of one's own strength and to totally depend on God for His help, healing, and guidance.

He couldn't understand the betrayal, the wound, the tragedy to himself, which this dark, horrible event had brought into his life, so he turned it all over to the Lord, **as he died to self.** In Romans 6:11, Paul states,

"Likewise reckon ye also yourselves to be dead indeed unto sin, but alive unto God through Jesus Christ our Lord."

"Then said Jesus unto his disciples, 'If any man will come after me, let him deny himself, and take up his cross (his work), *and follow me'"* (Matthew 16:24). David is not talking about dying and going to heaven as a saint (child of God), he is declaring his abandonment of self (his will and desires) and totally surrendering to the Lord.

PSALM 116:16

"O LORD, truly I am thy servant; I am thy servant, and the son of thine handmaid: thou hast loosed my bonds." David states twice that he is the servant of God. He is referring to his surrender to God; then he declares the MARVELOUS RESULTS OF HIS DEATH TO SELF (surrender). God **loosed David's bonds of bitterness** that were holding him prisoner and destroying his life. When David died to self, his hurt and pain were gone. His heartbroken condition was gone. He was free! **God loosed his bonds.** God set him free from his bitterness.

PSALM 116:17

"I will offer to thee the sacrifice of thanksgiving, and will call upon the name of the LORD." David is now filled with God's healing and gives thanksgiving to God. He tells us that he will continue to call upon the name of the Lord as he follows the Lord and walks by faith.

PSALM 116:18

"I will pay my vows unto the LORD now in the presence of all his people." David is going to tell everyone how good, understanding and great God is. **Man hurts, but God heals**, and David now wants everyone to look to Jesus and receive the same peace and healing that he has obtained. David is proclaiming that life is full and joyful again.

PSALM 116:19

"In the courts of the LORD'S house, in the midst of thee, O Jerusalem. Praise ye the LORD." David expands his declaration by telling everyone in the Lord's house. Then he goes further by stating that he will tell the whole city.

PSALM 117

In Psalm 117, he expands his desire from telling the local people, to telling the whole world (all people): *"O praise the LORD, all ye nations: praise him, all ye people. For his merciful kindness is great toward us: and the truth of the LORD endureth for ever. Praise ye the LORD."* He concludes this Psalm with the same descriptive term, *"PRAISE YE THE LORD."*

Though this doesn't seem quite adequate to describe the praise, the joy, or the victory he has in letting God handle and bless his life, yet from **a healthy soul** he calls out, **"Praise ye the Lord!"**

Throughout Psalm 116 and 117, there are two principles God is stressing through David's experiences:

First, the "greatly afflicted" experience was **"merciful kindness"** in disguise. When David yielded to God for His guidance, God transformed David's hurts into healing and happiness.

Second, *"The truth of the Lord endureth forever"* is directed toward the help God gives to all those who will be "greatly afflicted" **in some future generation.**

In plain easy to understand language, David is saying, God is not a respector of persons. If He helped me, **He will help you,** because **His mercy endureth forever.**

DAVID'S CLOSING STATEMENT OF VICTORY
PSALM 116:17-19

"I will offer to thee the sacrifice of praise,"

"I will call upon the name of the Lord"
(ask His guidance),

"I will pay my vows unto the Lord now in the presence of all his people" (serve God faithfully),

"I will pay my vows in the courts of the Lord's house, in the midst of thee, O Jerusalem"
(go to church faithfully),

"I will praise the Lord."

D avid is not only praising the Lord in the Lord's presence, but he is praising the Lord to all the people of Israel and to all the nations (v. 1). David is grateful that **his affliction was merciful kindness in disguise** and that God's truth endureth forever (v. 2).

THE HIGH ROAD

David took the high road to victory, success and peace. Others take the low road to continual pain and problems. The name of David shines brightly, while the names of others are soon forgotten. Don't you see that the right choice is the one David made? Wouldn't you like to join David in saying, "Praise the Lord!" Study carefully the remainder of this book and you will be able to join him on the **"Road to Victory!"**

POINTS TO PONDER

- Psalm 116 shows that there is deep conviction of sin before one is saved.

- Every person will have heartbreaking experiences and offenses in life.

- How one responds to these offenses, will depend on his relationship with God.

- David's decision was to die to self and fully keep his commitment to God. This decision brought much joy to David and praise constantly flowed from his lips.

- Salvation brings peace and security, as well as, a deep appreciation of God.

- Surrender, total surrender to Christ, brings unspeakable joy, like a fountain of living water bubbling up from within.

- One cannot cross from salvation to this joyful life that Jesus described as the abundant life, **unless he crosses over the bridge of testing, trouble, and tears.**

- Most people stay on the bank of existence, suffering, pain and disenchantment.

- This book was written to show a person **how to cross over the bridge** and then encourage him to join others who are walking on the ROAD TO VICTORY AND GLORY.

LESSON FOR CHAPTER ONE

MONDAY
(PSALM 116:1-9)

1. He found _____ and _____ as he wrestled with his _____ and _____ condition.

2. This _____ lost condition caused David to _____ out to God and ask God to _____ him.

3. Since the Lord has dealt _____ with him, his soul has found _____ and forgiveness.

4. *"For Thou has _____ my soul from _____, mine eyes from _____, and my feet from falling."*

5. *"I will _____ before the Lord in the _____ of the living."*

TUESDAY
(PSALM 116:10-12)

1. When he began to _____ and share his _____ in his Savior, it _____.

2. David came to the place where he believed that
   _____ was a hypocrite and a _____.

3. He was _____ and hungry, greatly afflicted
   and _____ confused.

4. How was he going to handle this _____ and
   his _____ service to the Lord?

5. He _____ take his anger out on _____.

WEDNESDAY
(PSALM 116:13-15)

1. *"I will take the _____ of _____, and call
   upon the _____ of the Lord."*

2. *"Calling upon the name of the Lord"* was the
   _____ step of David as he started on the
   "Road to Victory!"

3. He would continue _____ to church
   _____ and serving God.

4. He is referring to the _____ of his wants, his
   desires and his _____ will.

5. He is _____ his abandonment of self and
   totally _____ to the Lord.

THURSDAY
(PSALM 116:16-19)

1. *"O Lord, truly I am thy _____: I am Thy _____."*

2. God loosed David's bonds of _____, that were holding him _____ and destroying his life.

3. David is going to tell everyone how _____ and _____ and _____ God is.

4. Man _____, but God _____.

5. Then he _____ further by stating that he will tell the _____ city.

FRIDAY
(PSALM 117)

1. He concludes this Psalm with the _____ descriptive term, "_____ ye the Lord."

2. First, the "greatly afflicted" experience was "_____" in disguise.

3. David is saying, God is _____ a respecter of persons.

4. David was _____ that his _____ was merciful kindness in _____.

5. Study _____ the remainder of this book and you will be able to _____ him on the **"Road to Victory!"**

COMMITMENT TO EXCELLENCE

Having studied this lesson, I now have a better understanding of how to face adversity in my life and I will strive to face each problem with faith in God.

_____   _____

Name   Date

DAILY FAITH BUILDER

CHAPTER ONE

DAILY DECLARATION:

I will major on **God's promises** and minimize life's problems. **Repeat this phrase aloud each morning and evening.**

MEMORY VERSE:

"Precious in the sight of the LORD is the death of his saints" (Psalm 116:15).

CHECK BLOCK AFTER REPEATING

Mon	Tues	Wed	Thurs	Fri	Sat	Sun
A.M.						
P.M.						

Grade: _____

Is the parent responsible for all the bad
that his child does?

Is the husband responsible for the wife's
spending of the family's money which was?

Then Why Blame God?

Chapter Two

CHAPTER TWO

THREE REACTIONS TO HEARTBREAK AND OFFENSE

*F*ollowing are **three different reactions** to heartbreak and offense. Everyone will react to the severe problems of life in one of three ways:

I WAS *"GREATLY AFFLICTED"*

"My baby died!"

"My sister was killed in a car wreck!"

"My precious sweet mother was murdered!"

"My handsome and moral teenage son, who was going to be a preacher, was killed in an accident!"

These are a few of the different heartbreaks that one might experience in life. They can occur naturally, or they can be used **by the devil to cause anger toward God.** This anger, unchecked, turns to bitterness and ends in the self-destruction of an individual.

Everyone in the human race at some point in his lifetime **will experience** heartbreak, sickness, death of a loved one, or rejection by a parent, spouse, child or friend. Some of these experiences will be so devastating, that they will cause a person to **want to die**. It will seem easier to "just die," give up on life, than go on. LIFE IS NOT FAIR! Many times you will not get a fair shake. Probably, some of these experiences have "greatly afflicted" you. You might say as David said, *"All men are liars."* Yes, heartbreak and offence will affect each of us at some time in our lives.

How to Make Bad Things Turn Out for Good

The heart of David's message in Psalm 116, shows us how to react to heartbreak properly. **That is the reason the Holy Spirit placed this Psalm in the Bible.** The important truth to learn, is how to make these bad experiences **work for your good.**

1. "I Quit!"

The first group of people say, "I Quit!" They throw up their hands and never go back to church again. They Quit! They quit church, they quit God by saying, "If this is Christianity, I don't want any part of it. I've had it! I'm through. I Quit!"

2. "I Quit, But I Can't Quit!"

The second group of people say, "I Quit, But I Can't Quit!" A woman may want to quit, but she is married to a pastor. A man would quit, but he can't quit, all his family and friends go to church. His whole life revolves around moral, church going people. The phrase they are using, "I quit, but I can't quit!" means that in their hearts they quit, even though they still attend church services. **They determine never to let anyone hurt them again.** They build a wall around their hearts and refuse to reach out to others – they are spiritually wounded. They continue going to church **by covering up** the wound and concealing their feelings. They refuse to **let people see** that they are really hurting inside. It's a shame, because those people may be the very ones that God could use to help them. They still go on outwardly, but inwardly, "they quit!"

3. "I QUIT" BY DYING TO SELF

The third group has learned to die to self and turn their heartbreaks over to God. Their reaction to being hurt is what we see in Psalm 116. David reacted to the terrible blows which he received in his cruel world, by turning it all over to God. **He confessed to God that he didn't understand it. It hurt so bad, that he couldn't bare it. He recalled how sinful and unworthy he was before he was saved and no one could help him. Then he asked the Lord to help him and trusted Jesus as his Savior.** Jesus was the only one who could help him in his lost condition. David cried out to God in his despair and God saved him. Now, in his wounded, afflicted condition, there was only one thing left for him to do – **turn it all over to Jesus – dying to his own self, his own understanding and his own effort.** When he did that, the bonds of hurt and bitterness melted away. **He became a free man.** He now became a man on his way to living a victorious life.

"ALL THINGS WORK TOGETHER FOR GOOD"

*T*he effect of the unspeakable joy and victory in the life of David is affirming, *"And we know that all things work together for good to them that love God, to them who are the called according to his purpose"* (Romans 8:28). Life's problems along with God's solutions also testify that *"For our light affliction, which is but for a moment, worketh for us a far more exceeding and eternal weight of glory"* (II Corinthians 4:17). Compared to eternity, our light affliction (the ordeals and problems we suffer), is but for a moment. These trials were designed to equip us to be better servants on God's behalf to mankind and to give us a greater place and position in eternity.

Is the family responsible for the action
which some of the relatives plot?

Is the city council responsible for the
accident in the Supermarket's parking lot??

Then Why Blame God?

Chapter Three

CHAPTER THREE

THE END RESULT FROM EACH "I QUIT!"

1. THE END RESULT OF "I QUIT!"

Through the years, as I knocked on doors, I met people who professed to be Christians and who were basically good, moral people; however, they had quit going to church. I would do everything in my power to get them back in church, but almost without exception, **I failed.** Back in the background of these dear people's lives were similar dark experiences, which they allowed to cause them TO QUIT!

THE EFFECTS OF QUITTING
UPON THREE GENERATIONS

*T*here is a story in the Old Testament which perfectly illustrates the cause of offense and the horrible, eternal results of quitting! This is the story of three kings of Judah.

Grandpa Uzziah Was "Greatly Afflicted"

The First Generation. II Chronicles 26:11-20 tells the story of the grandpa, Uzziah. Uzziah reigned for a period of 52 years in Jerusalem. He did right in the sight of the Lord, as his father had and as long as he continued to seek God, **God prospered him.** However, his heart became so proud that he became corrupted and was unfaithful to the Lord his God. **Uzziah began to walk in the flesh** and became so bold, that he took it upon himself to enter the temple to burn his own incense upon the altar of incense. **The priests rebuked and opposed the king** and told him that he was not to be in that area of the temple. While Uzziah was standing there enraged at the priests for stopping him, **the Lord struck him with leprosy** and he had to live in a separate house until the day of his death.

Jotham, the Son, Quit Church

The Second Generation. II Chronicles 27:1-9 continues the story with the father, Jotham. Jotham was the son of Uzziah and upon his father's death, became the king of Judah. The Bible teaches that Jotham knew the Lord and was a good, godly man. *"Jotham grew mighty because he ordered his ways before the Lord his God; however, he never entered the temple."* Through the disgrace of his father's open punishment by God, **JOTHAM QUIT.** HE NEVER AGAIN ENTERED THE TEMPLE (church). In his heart, he must have said, "I

Quit," because he never darkened the door of the temple again. He reigned for 16 years and died and his son Ahaz became king.

AHAZ, THE GRANDSON, WENT TO HELL

The Third Generation. II Chronicles 28:1-27. The son Ahaz, grandson of Uzziah, reign in Judah for 16 years in his father, Jotham's place. However, this young man of 20 years of age, walked in the ways of the kings of Israel. He burned incense on the high places, desecrated articles of the temple and **closed the doors** to the house of the Lord. Therefore, Ahaz was delivered by the Lord into the hands of the king of Aram (Assyria), which afflicted him with heavy casualties. **Ahaz never was saved,** and he was a very wicked, ungodly person who **died and went to hell.**

THE VIVID CONSEQUENCES OF "I QUIT"

The stories of these three kings (grandpa, father and son), show the vivid results that happen when a person does not deal properly when "greatly afflicted." Their lives show that every one who allows adversities to cause them to quit, will become a stumbling block to their families and friends. Their own grandchildren will stumble over them and they, the ones who quit, will be responsible for **sending their own flesh and blood to hell.** What a horrible consequence for quitting!

2. THE END RESULT OF "I QUIT, BUT I CAN'T QUIT"

"Johnny, sit down!" was the order that the mother gave to her five-year-old son who was standing up in his chair. No response from Johnny. **"Johnny, sit down!!"** yelled the mother. Johnny sat down, but under his breath he murmured, "I'M SITTING DOWN, BUT IN MY MIND, I'M STILL STANDING UP!" This illustration shows what many of God's children are doing. They can't quit going to church for one reason or another, but in their minds, they echo their true feelings, "I Quit!"

THEY BECOME THE WALKING WOUNDED

They have a problem. They are good people, but because they want their peers, bosses and fellow associates to like and respect them, **they hide their hurt and true feelings** by acting pleasant. They are friendly, likable and popular on the outside, but their true condition is that they have become "THE WALKING WOUNDED."

They are well thought of by the church members and are respected by the pastor. All that they, those who are "greatly afflicted," allow the people at church to see, **is their outward face,** which is generally smiling and happy.

One lady reasons to herself, "I would quit, but I can't quit, because I married the pastor." A man inwardly thinks, "I would quit, but I can't quit because **I am the pastor.**"

Another person reasons, "Church is my life, all my family and friends are there. I like them, so I can't quit, but in my heart I vow, '**No one will ever hurt me again.**' I quit, but I won't quit attending."

The problem identified. The problem with a person who quits on the inside, is that **they can't always portray** an up-beat, happy outward disposition, because in their hearts they are hurting. Sometimes when they are sick or just tired and worn out, **they will let their guard down.** When this happens, they will slip and someone will see just how unhappy they are. **Their true feelings, the bitterness, the years of hurt will come flooding out of their mouths.**

Where does this generally happen? AT HOME.

Who generally gets their ugly vomit spewed out all over them? **Their children and other family members.** Then the bitterness, resentment and frustration from their hurt spirit, is transferred **to the minds of their children.**

The children begin to drop out of church and in their teenage years, turn away from Christ completely. **The children become crippled Christians at best,** or at the worst, rebellious, non-going, anti-church adults. Their example becomes a stumbling block to everyone around them. **Some who carry this hidden, wounded spirit around with them,** will also cause **many of their grandchildren** to go to hell!

3. "I QUIT" BY DYING TO SELF

The Third Reaction is dying to self and turning the heartbreak over to God. The often jailed, beaten, lied about, and misunderstood Apostle Paul confessed, "I die daily." He also stated, *"I am crucified with Christ: nevertheless I live; yet not I, but Christ liveth in me: and the life which I now live in the flesh I live by the faith of the Son of God, who loved me, and gave himself for me. I do not frustrate the grace of God"* (Galatians 2:20-21). Paul showed his complete surrender to God and his understanding of how God can make *"all things work together for good to them that love God"* (Romans 8:28) in his life. Paul is talking about a true Christian in his Roman letter.

PAUL SHOCKED THE WORLD

*P*aul wrote, *"We glory in **tribulations** also: knowing that tribulation worketh patience; And patience, experience; and experience, hope: And hope maketh not ashamed; because the love of God is shed abroad in our hearts by the Holy Ghost which is given unto us"* (Romans 5:3-5). Simply stated, we are blessed and obtain experience, comfort and the grace of God, as we go through tribulations (trouble). This experience makes us better Christians, who gain a greater knowledge of God and how to minister and help others. Therefore, **Paul taught that we can learn to praise God** for the horrible problems and experiences that come upon us.

THE OLD BRIDGE BUILDER

*E*veryone has heard the story of the old bridge builder who turned aside to build **the bridge over the chasm wide.** When asked why, the old bridge builder replied, "It is for the benefit of the lad who is following. This chasm wide may have been his downfall."

When you go through a heartbreak, it could be your "Chasm Wide," but if you don't let it beat you, you will learn that it was for the benefit of someone who needed your experience and encouragement to salvage his life. Then in return, in some future experience, they will be able to overcome some "great afflictions" and continue to serve God. REMEMBER! **Life is your school and you are continually being taught by Jesus, through the Holy Spirit who is your personal teacher.**

JESUS, YOUR TEACHER, WILL TAKE YOUR HAND

*T*he next time you are down in the valley of depression and fear, "greatly afflicted," and you seem to be all alone, remember Jesus, your school teacher, is with you and promises **never to leave nor forsake you.** The difficult lesson you are learning, will cause you to rejoice later. It will also be for your eternal glory. *"But the God of all grace, who hath called us UNTO HIS ETERNAL GLORY by Christ Jesus, after that ye have suffered a while, make you perfect, stablish, strengthen, settle you"* (I Peter 5:10). **God will take you by the hand** and safely lead you through the dark valley to a future "golden daybreak." Learn to trust Him because He is your friend and He will safely lead you through the darkest of nights.

POINTS TO PONDER

♦ Some people quit, but can never really quit, because they are held CAPTIVE OF THE PAST.

♦ Some people quit, but they can't really quit, because they live a religious life. They become the walking wounded, who sow bitterness in the lives of their families DESTROYING THEIR FUTURES.

♦ Some people quit by dying to self, which causes them to eagerly LIVE FOR TODAY with God's eternal blessings ENRICHING THEIR LIVES.

♦ Each individual must decide for himself which of the following paths to take:

- he can become A CAPTIVE OF THE PAST and let his life become unproductive,
- he can become DESTRUCTIVE IN THE FUTURE by harboring his hurts and wounds, which will destroy his life and possibly those around him, or
- he can choose to live a happy DAILY LIFE, right now, which will bring fruitfulness and joy.

LESSON FOR CHAPTERS TWO AND THREE

MONDAY
(I WAS "GREATLY AFFLICTED")

1. My precious sweet _____ was murdered.

2. This anger, _____, turns to _____ and ends in the self-destruction of an individual.

3. Life is not _____. Many _____ you will _____ get a fair shake.

4. David's _____ in Psalm 116 shows us how to _____ to heartbreak properly.

5. The _____ truth to _____ is how to make these bad _____ work for your good.

TUESDAY
("I QUIT" – ALL THINGS WORK)

1. They throw up their _____ and never go back to _____ again.

2. A woman may want to _____, but she is married to the _____.

3. They refuse to _____ people _____ that they are really _____ inside.

4. The _____ group has learned to _____ to _____ and turn their heartbreaks over to God.

5. These trials were _____ to equip us to be better _____.

WEDNESDAY
("I QUIT" – THEY BECOME THE WALKING WOUNDED)

1. There is a story in the _____ Testament which _____ illustrates the cause of the offense and the horrible, _____ results of quitting.

2. Ahaz never was _____ and was a very wicked and ungodly person who died and _____ to Hell.

3. Their own _____ will stumble over them.

4. Sometime when they are _____ or just tired and worn out, they let their _____ down.

5. Their _____ become crippled Christians at _____ or at the worst, rebellious, non-going, anti-church adults.

THURSDAY
("I QUIT" BY DYING TO SELF)

1. The _____ reaction to dying to _____ and turning the heartbreak over to _____.

2. The often jailed, beaten, lied about and misunderstood Apostle Paul confessed, "*I _____ daily.*"

3. "*I am _____ with Christ; nevertheless, I live.*"

4. God can make "_____ *things work together for* _____ *to them that love God.*"

5. Paul is talking about a _____ Christian in his Roman letter.

FRIDAY
(PAUL SHOCKED THE WORLD)

1. We are blessed and _____ experience, _____ and the grace of God as we _____ through tribulations.

2. Paul taught that we can learn to praise God for the _____ problems and _____ that come upon us.

3. It is for the _____ of the _____ who is following.

4. Life is your school and you are _____ being taught by Jesus, who is your personal _____.

5. God will take you by the _____ and _____ lead you _____ the dark valley to a future "golden daybreak."

COMMITMENT TO EXCELLENCE

Having studied the horrible consequences of QUITTING, I now seek God's help in overcoming all of my heartbreaks and problems.

_____   _____

Name   Date

DAILY FAITH BUILDER

CHAPTERS TWO AND THREE

DAILY DECLARATION:

The well-being of all the lives of my family depend on my healthy relationship with God. **Repeat this phrase aloud each morning and evening**.

MEMORY VERSE:

"But seek ye first the kingdom of God, and his righteousness; and all these things shall be added unto you" (Matthew 6:33).

CHECK BLOCK AFTER REPEATING

Mon	Tues	Wed	Thurs	Fri	Sat	Sun
A.M.						
P.M.						

Grade: _____

Can we fault the highway patrolman
out on the Interstate for all the
speeding cars driven by
people running late?

Then Why Blame God?

Chapter Four

CHAPTER FOUR

GOD'S LOVE AND PURPOSE FOR ALLOWING PROBLEMS

*N*otice that God loves you and has a purpose for **allowing problems** in the lives of His children. Most of the time God does not cause the problem, but He does allow it. Many times, after He has put up roadblocks to keep the tragedy from happening, He allows it to happen.

God tries to prevent the tragedy by sending thoughts of caution into the person's mind, which the person ignores.

God causes a concerned person, such as a parent, pastor, or friend, to give advice that would have greatly limited the hurt the person would experience, but the person pays little or no attention to it. **Then the heartbreak happens!**

The main cause of the problem **is the devil.** However, each individual person **has to allow** the devil to work within him, in order for the devil to succeed. Most people deny the existence of the devil, therefore, they fail to recognize his subtle attacks.

The devil's favorite stumbling block is to cause a horrible problem to the person or the death of his loved one. The devil then **plants his lie into the mind** of the one affected, steps back and **lets the person blame God** for it.

The devil's second favorite stumbling block, is to shoot all types of rebellious or lustful thoughts into a person's mind. Then, **he plants the lie in that person's** mind that the person is weak and **no-good**. These sinful thoughts are instigated by the devil, but if the person fails to brush them out of his mind, the devil will build on them until the person sins, **thus allowing the devil to be successful**.

HIT ME AGAIN, DEVIL

We actually reveal our "Achilles heel" or our "glass jaw" to the devil, when he discovers that all he has to do is bring on hard times, tragic loss, sickness, depression, or lust (some of the devil's many devices) and **we will fold up and automatically doubt God**. He will continue to **repeat** this attack time after time in our lives.

THREE REASONS "YOU," AS A MEMBER OF THE HUMAN RACE, HAVE TRAGEDIES

We will attempt to help hurting people cope with their problem by identifying the most common causes for heartbreak and problems.

1. YOU ARE A HUMAN BEING

The fact that you are a human being is one of the main reasons you have problems.

We are God's creatures who are on this earth in a physical body for a limited, uncertain time. As such, we all have

sicknesses,

disappointments,

physical and mental pain,

separations,

heartbreaks,

tears,

and death.

There is nothing that happens to any of us, which couldn't happen to all of us.

The shortened summary of life by the inspired writer Job, is *"Man that is born of women is of few days, and full of trouble"* (Job 14:1).

As a member of the human race, you must learn to cope with problems, adversities, sickness and death, because that is what the human race is all about. **Trouble, sickness, disappointment and death!**

2. You Are Made in the Image and Likeness of God, and the Devil Hates You!

Whether you understand this heading or not, it's true. The devil so totally hates God, that you as a member of the human race, made in God's image, become the blunt of his attacks.

God loves man and since the devil cannot touch God, he spends all his time hurting and destroying man in his effort **to hurt God.** Think about how any good parent hurts when their child is harmed and you will understand why the devil hurts human beings.

Don't Get Angry at God

For many people, it is too late to admonish them not to get angry at God, because **that is already their problem. They are angry with God!** They may not acknowledge it or even recognize it, but that **is** their problem: **They are blaming God for their hurt!**

READ ABOUT THE COMPASSION OF GOD

Please stop and read about the love and ministry of Jesus. He came as God in the flesh. As God, He demonstrated **His tenderness, compassion** and **love** toward hurting people. Read all the accounts of His ministry which are found in the books of Matthew, Mark, Luke and John.

Can you find ONE PLACE in the gospels where Jesus ever refused to help anyone who was lonely or hurting? Is there even ONE EXAMPLE of His being cold or indifferent toward the needs of a person regardless of his sinfulness or status in life?

THERE ARE NONE

Search as you may and you will not find one conduct of neglect, coldness, or indifference in which you can accuse God. In fact, the opposite is true. You will find God (through Jesus) going to great length to comfort, heal and save as many people as will LET Him.

There is a Devil

Who causes all the distortions of God in your mind? Who changes the loving God, found in the Bible, into the cold, indifferent God, that you visualize in your mind? **It is literally the devil** who hates you and tries to destroy you. He is real and takes people captive by distorting their views of God in their minds. Each Christian must seek the truth of the Bible and not give in to their thoughts and imaginations. *"And that they may recover themselves out of the snare of the devil, who are taken captive by him at his will"* (II Timothy 2:26). "At his will?" That seems so assuming and arrogant; like we are only child's play and easy prey. Don't let it be so! God admonishes us to, *"Resist the devil, and he will flee from you"* (James 4:7).

Bible Commands

The Apostle Paul tells of the wiles (methods) of the devil in Ephesians 6:11. He commands Christians to, *"Put on the whole armour of God, that ye may be able to stand against the wiles of the devil."* He even commands people to use the promises in the Bible to quench all the fiery darts (thoughts), which the devil shoots into their minds. *"Above all, taking the shield of faith, wherewith ye shall be able to quench all the fiery darts of the wicked"* (v. 16).

In another scripture, Paul commands the believer to pull down strongholds (imaginations), that the devil has built up in the person's mind. He tells him to bring every thought into the obedience of Christ and the Bible. *"(For the weapons of our warfare are not carnal, but mighty through God to the pulling down of strong holds;) Casting down **imaginations**, and **every high thing that exalteth itself against the knowledge of God,** and **bringing into captivity every thought to the obedience of Christ"** (II Corinthians 10:4-5).

GOD'S MASTERFUL ILLUSTRATION

Most of the world believes that there is a God, yet they do not believe in a literal devil.

The devil does all the dirty work and **God is blamed for it**. God becomes the villain, because people reason in their minds, "How could a loving God allow little children to be abused, to starve to death, or receive inhumane treatment by their own parents?" And so it goes, the devil causes war, destruction and death, and **God is blamed for it**. Before we get to God's masterful plan to identify the monster behind all their tragedies, may we give the truth as presented in the Bible.

JOHN 10:10

Jesus said, *"The thief cometh not, but for to steal, and to kill, and to destroy..."* That's what the devil does. He is behind every alienation from parents, every broken

55

promise which leads to divorce through outside forces, and the stealing away of love and affection. He is behind every heartbreak that murder, war and death brings. He is behind the destruction of every thing that is decent and good. He is the devil, the destroyer of dreams, lives and people.

JESUS CAME TO GIVE LIFE

"I am come that they might have life, and that they might have it more abundantly." This is the last half of verse 10, which tells us that Jesus came to give life instead of death. Jesus gives meaning to life, so that people can cope with all the attacks of the devil and live a victorious life of peace and fruitfulness.

WHO'S THE VILLAIN?

The devil is the god of this age (our present age) and has the power of death and destruction.

Jesus is coming back to the earth as the conquering King of Kings to rule and reign for one thousand years. As He begins His reign over the earth, **the first thing He will do, is bind the devil and put him into the bottomless pit (Hell), and there will be peace, harmony and happiness during this period of one thousand years.** This is exactly what the world would be like today if there was no devil. Always remember that.

God's Masterful Demonstration

After Jesus' reign of one thousand years, the devil is let out of prison (the bottomless pit) **for a short time.** As soon as he is back on earth, he will deceive the nations again and there will be war, rebellion, death and all manner of trouble again.

It is Plain to See

When you view God's mighty illustration, which is one thousand years of total peace, it is clear that **it is not God,** but the devil, who is responsible for all the heartaches and pain that the human race is suffering.

God, Why Let Him Out?

I used to wonder, "God, why will you let him out, once you have him in hell? When you have him there, keep him there," was my reasoning. Think with me for a minute and you will discover through God's masterful illustration, why God let the devil out for a brief period and **who the real villain is**.

Before the devil is placed in hell, **the earth is full of violence, wars, death** and **total confusion.**

When the devil is in hell for the one thousand years, there will be love, peace and harmony between the races.

57

There will not be any sickness, wars, death, divorces, killings, thievery, or disruptions of any kind. Total peace and tranquility will rule on the earth!

So you see, letting the devil out of hell for this short period of time, is **God's way of proving a point.** That point is, that **it is the devil** which initiates evil, destruction and death. God is the one who gives grace, help and aid to the victims if they will only let Him. Think about it; then **read the poem on page 71.**

3. THE HURTS WILL BE TURNED INTO HELPS, IF YOU WILL ALLOW THEM TO

There are many people whose experiences were recorded in the Bible, who turned to God and were able to grow, because of the hurts they experienced. I will refer to three prominent characters of the Bible and their grievous experiences.

DAVID'S HURTS WERE TURNED INTO HELPS

David suffered the loss of all things in just a few days. He went from royalty, to fugitive and from being at home with his loving bride, to being divorced while in exile. Yet, after he turned his problem over to God and died to self, his song became a continual *"Praise the Lord!"*

JOSEPH'S HURTS WERE TURNED INTO HELPS

As a teenage boy, Joseph could only dream of helping his family. But, as the most powerful man under the king, he could shelter and care for his whole nation.

The hurts he had for over a decade of his life, prepared him to live the rest of his life as the patriot and hero of Israel. You'll find a more complete look at Joseph's life in Chapter Five.

PAUL'S HURTS WERE TURNED INTO HELPS

A reader of the New Testament will recognize that the Apostle Paul endured more pain and suffering, than any other person written about in the Bible. But, as we read the last epistle that he wrote while an inmate in prison, we hear a joyful, happy man. A man who is rejoicing in the fact that God had turned all his hurts into helps and had greatly enriched his ministry because of it. One can almost hear Paul shout as he wrote his victorious statement in II Timothy 4:6-8, "*I have fought a good fight, I have finished my course, I have kept the faith. Henceforth and there is lay up for me a crown...*" Further information on Paul's victory can be found in Chapter Five.

YOUR HURTS CAN ALSO BECOME HELPS

Are you in the midst of a trial or heartbreak? God is not a respecter of persons, and **He loves you.** Empty your heart of unforgiveness and bitterness and let Him bring you through your dark night into the bright day of success and victory.

WITHOUT FORM AND VOID OF BEAUTY

The God who made this beautiful earth from a world, *"without form and void"* (Genesis 1:2), can certainly reshape your life into a life of peace and blessing. He will do it, if you will only confess your hurts and trust Him to heal you. God is waiting!

WHY DO THE GOOD DIE AND THE BAD LIVE?

Many people are greatly troubled over the death of a good person who has not lived a full lifetime. They begin to question God by saying, **"It isn't fair for such a wonderful, caring, productive person to die** and for 'that creature' to live." "That creature" is normally some derelict or criminal who mistreats and dishonors his family. The loss of a righteous person is very hard to take when it is your parent, son, daughter, or another loved one. Please consider the following for encouragement.

ALL MUST DIE

Actually, the statement that "the good die, while the bad live," is not a true statement. All men die, whether they are good or bad. But there are a lot of questions, particularly in the minds of the loved ones of a Christian person who dies suddenly.

WHY DO THE SAVED DIE SUDDENLY?

DELIVERED FROM AN EVIL TO COME. *"The righteous perisheth, and no man layeth it to heart: and merciful men are taken away, none considering that the righteous is taken away from the evil to come. He shall enter into peace: they shall rest in their beds, each one walking in his uprightness"* (Isaiah 57:1-2). Consider these two verses as an explanation for such tragedies. *"The righteous man perisheth (dies)."* **A righteous man is a saved man.** *"Merciful men are taken away."* **Merciful men are active Christians showing love and winning others to Christ.** They are trying to live their lives as an example to others and working to fulfill God's commands.

In verse two, *"they shall rest in their beds,"* is an ancient colloquialism which means, they have died and gone to be with their fathers. In other words, this righteous and merciful man dies and his body is dressed for his burial and placed in the bedroom of his home. All his family and friends view the body before it is laid to rest (buried by his loved ones). *"His spirit has entered into peace"* (gone to heaven) with all of his good works in tact, to be remembered and treasured by those left behind (surviving family and friends).

The good memories of the deceased will be used of God to encourage and motivate his loved ones and friends. PLEASE NOTE THE REASON FOR THIS PERSON'S UNTIMELY ACCIDENT OR DEATH. *"That the righteous is taken away from the evil to come"* (v. 1). God saw a problem – a sin or an evil experience – laying in the path of that righteous one, which could turn him away from God into a life which would have destroyed his testimony; hindering his family and friends and the cause of Christ. SO GOD IN HIS MERCY, REACHED DOWN AND TOOK THAT PERSON FROM THE EVIL TO COME. God lifted his spirit to heaven, leaving his good name and his testimony unscathed. It was an act of mercy, kindness and love on the part of God; not one of unconcern or of punishment.

JESUS ALWAYS DID THE RIGHT THING

*J*esus gave His life on the cross in order to provide for a person's future good. Jesus didn't come to destroy the world, **but to save it.** *"For God sent not his Son into the world to condemn the world; but that the world through him might be saved"* (John 3:17). Throughout the whole account of his life on the earth, Jesus was the friend and tender-hearted comforter. He showed love, compassion and tenderness to all. He always made life better, He lifted the heavy burdens from the weary travelers backs. **He always did the right thing!** Now, in the death of your precious loved one, HE DID THE BEST THING FOR HIM. He lifted the person up to heaven from some horrible EVIL to come.

EVILS TO COME

Evils to come may be extreme:

- abuse by a parent, spouse, or stranger,
- pain and suffering caused by a crippling disease,
- a sudden death,
- a heartbreaking accident, or
- a hurt caused by a friend or loved one.

These evils can cause pain to others, can warp a person's outlook and even ruin his life or end it. Regardless of what "the evil" may be, God allowed the evil to work for the good of the one who was hurt or the deceased and not for his harm or hurt. It may even be for the good of someone near and dear to him.

YOU CAN TRUST THE MAN WHO DIED FOR YOU!

You don't know the future, **but God does.** Can you consider that in the death of your loved one, that God allowed him to escape from something that may have been far worse for him than death? Some horrible catastrophe, sorrow, pain or suffering to himself: something that would have caused him to lose spiritually; or maybe it was to keep him from becoming a stumbling block to someone else?

While we were **yet sinners,** Jesus died for us. While we were **yet rebellious,** Jesus died for us. Now, if you can't trust the man who died for you, **WHO CAN YOU TRUST?**

"The righteous perisheth, and no man layeth it to heart: and merciful men are taken away, none considering that the righteous is taken away from the evil to come" (Isaiah 57:1). This verse teaches that God takes some very good people from an evil to come, something that they would not be able to handle or bear.

So, turn your problems over to Jesus, **He always does the right thing!**

POINTS TO PONDER

♦ One has suffering, because he is a member of the human race. *"Man that is born of woman is of few days, and full of trouble"* (Job 14:1).

♦ One has suffering, because he is made in the image of God and the devil's way of hurting God is to afflict God's children.

♦ One has suffering, because God allows it and promises to make it work out for the person's good, if the person will allow Him.

♦ God promises never to leave or forsake His children, for He is the God of all Grace.

♦ God even allows some good people to suffer for their eternal good.

♦ God even allows some good people to die prematurely, because He is sheltering them from "evil to come."

♦ **God is good and He always does the RIGHT thing!**

LESSON FOR CHAPTER FOUR

MONDAY
(GOD'S LOVE AND PURPOSE FOR ALLOWING AFFLICTIONS)

1. Notice that God _____ you and has a purpose for _____ problems in the lives of His children.

2. He sends _____ of caution into the person's _____ that the person _____.

3. The main _____ of the problem is the _____.

4. The devil's _____ favorite stumbling block is to _____ a horrible problem or death.

5. We will help hurting _____ cope with their _____ by identifying the most common causes.

TUESDAY
(YOU ARE A HUMAN BEING)

1. The _____ that you are a _____ being is one of the main reasons you have problems.

2. *"Man that is born of* _____ *is of few*
   _____ *, and full of trouble"* (Job 14:1).

3. Since the devil cannot _____ God, he spends
   all his time hurting and destroying man in his
   efforts to _____ God.

4. That is their _____; they are _____
   God for their hurt.

5. He was God demonstrating His _____,
   _____, and love toward _____ people.

WEDNESDAY
(THERE IS NONE – JOHN 10:10)

1. You will find God going to great _____ to
   comfort, heal and save as many people as will let Him.

2. Who _____ the loving God, found in the
   Bible into the _____, _____ God,
   which you visualize in your mind?

3. Paul tells of the _____ (methods) of the devil.

4. The _____ does all the _____ work and
   God is _____ for it.

5. He is behind the _____ of _____ thing
   that is _____ and _____.

THURSDAY
(JESUS CAME TO GIVE LIFE – GOD, WHY?)

1. The last half of verse 10, tells us that _____ came to give _____ instead of _____.

2. He will bind the devil and put him in the _____ pit and there will be _____ and _____ and harmony during this period of one thousand years.

3. As soon as he is back on earth, there will be _____.

4. Letting the devil out of hell for a short period of time is God's way of _____ a point.

5. God is the one who gives _____, help, and aid to the _____ if they will only let Him.

FRIDAY
(DAVID'S HURTS WERE TURNED INTO HELPS)

1. He went from royalty, to fugitive and from being at home with his loving _____, to being divorced while in _____.

2. The _____ he had for over a _____ of his life, prepared him to live the rest of his life as a _____ and hero of Israel.

3. He can certainly reshape your _____ into a life of _____ and blessing.

4. So God in His _____, reached down and took that person from the _____ to come.

5. In the death of your precious _____ one, He did the best _____ for him.

COMMITMENT TO EXCELLENCE

Having studied this lesson, I understand that God allows problems to happen to all. But the devil is behind all heartbreak and problems which God has determined to work for the good of those who love Him and allow Him to help.

_____   _____

Name   Date

DAILY FAITH BUILDER

CHAPTER FOUR

DAILY DECLARATION:

God, if you loved and helped others, you will surely help me. **Repeat this phrase aloud each morning and evening.**

MEMORY VERSE:

"For there is no difference between the Jew and the Greek: for the same Lord over all is rich unto all that call upon him" (Romans 10:12).

CHECK BLOCK AFTER REPEATING

Mon	Tues	Wed	Thurs	Fri	Sat	Sun
A.M.						
P.M.						

Grade: _____

Why Blame God?

Is the parent responsible for
all the bad that their child does?

Is a husband responsible for the wife's
impulsive spending of his money which was?

Is the family responsible for the action
which some of the relatives plot?

Is the city council responsible for the
accident in the Supermarket's parking lot?

Can we blame the family doctor who prescribes
to heal for the careless patient who fails to
take the prescribed pill?

Can we fault the highway patrolman out on
the Interstate for all the speeding cars
driven by people running late?

If you answer, "No" to all the
questions which are posed above,

Then, pray tell me, why do you **blame
your problems** on the God of love?

Why Do You Blame Your Problems
on the God of Love?

...Dr. James Wilkins

Chapter Five

CHAPTER FIVE

OTHERS WHO TRIUMPHED THROUGH THEIR AFFLICTIONS

*D*avid was the one God chose to teach us how to live through heartbreak and become victorious in our walk with Christ. In order to help us relate to David's example and apply it to our lives, let us consider four other examples:

1. The example of a 17-year-old kid,
2. The example of a broken-hearted mother,
3. The pain of the veteran missionary, and
4. The God of all grace.

THE FIRST EXAMPLE
A SEVENTEEN YEAR OLD KID

*I*n the book of Genesis, Chapters 30 through 47, it tells of Joseph's life. Joseph starts life as a happy kid, with spiritual insight, who loved to talk about

God! In his excitement of sharing about God's plans for his father's family, he angered his carnal (lost) brothers. One day in the back country, his brothers plotted his murder, took his prize possession (a coat of many colors), and threw him into a deep pit. One of his brothers, Judah, convinced the others to sell him into slavery instead of killing him.

How frightened and horrified this young seventeen year old must have been as his own brothers **heartlessly turned a deaf ear** to his pleas and sold him into a life of slavery.

A NATURAL CONCLUSION, "ALL MEN ARE LIARS"

In these trying and disappointing events, which transpired over the next twelve to thirteen years, Joseph could have echoed the same statement that David did, *"All men are liars."*

First, his own brothers betrayed him. **Second,** Potiphar's wife lied about this honest, loyal, hard-working young executive who was over her husband's business and had him thrown into prison. **Third,** the king's butler and baker forgot their promises, as Joseph languished in the federal penitentiary.

THE TRAINING PERIOD ENDED

God put Joseph in a carefully **orchestrated school for the first 30 years** of his life. During this period of preparation, there were many tears and long agonizing nights, as he lay in the prison irons, wondering about his uncertain future.

THIS GODLY MAN OF CONVICTION

Joseph entered into his years of trials as a happy, spiritual kid. He graduated as A BOLD MAN OF CONVICTION, who stood before Pharaoh, the most powerful king on the earth.

ONLY GOD KNEW THE DANGER

The great **God of heaven was the only one who knew** of the world-wide, seven years of famine, that would destroy most of the world, including God's chosen nation Israel. The way God chose to keep them from starving to death was **to move a seventeen year old boy several hundred miles and place him in a severe school of training.** This would bring Joseph to the attention of Pharaoh, the king of Egypt, where God's plan for survival and victory would unfold. **Burn this concept into your mind: only God knew the future tragedy that He was preparing Joseph to handle. Only God knows the future.**

THE PURPOSE FOR THE "GREATLY AFFLICTED"

Many years later, the brothers who sold him into slavery had to stand before Joseph (now the second most powerful man in the world), and they were greatly afraid of what he would do to them.

Joseph reassured his brothers, *"It was not you that sent me hither, but God"* (Genesis 45:8). Later, after the death of his father, Joseph comforted his brothers by saying, *"But as for you, **ye thought evil against me**; but God meant it unto good, to bring to pass, as it is this day, to save much people alive. Now therefore fear ye not: I will nourish you, and your little ones. And he comforted them, and spake kindly unto them"* (Genesis 50:20-21).

THE PLACE OF VICTORY

Joseph was lifted to one of the highest positions a Christian has ever attained. But the question arises, when was his actual day of victory? Some may explain, "Why, when the king placed his ring upon Joseph's finger; that was the time of his victory!" Oh no, my friend. The time of Joseph's victory took place years before the king's promotion. It could have been while he was stumbling alone as a boy with a slave-rope around his neck. It could have been later at Potiphar's house, or even while he was in prison, but it wasn't.

Joseph's victory took place when he believed God and died to self. *"Precious in the sight of the LORD is the death of his saints"* (Psalm 116:15). Joseph won the victory when the bonds of unforgiveness and bitterness were broken. This took place when, in spite of his environment and treatment, he turned his life over to God and trusted Him with the results. When he was exalted by Pharaoh, **it was only the outward demonstration of what had already taken place** in Joseph's life. In fact, there would never have been the great triumphs and victories in Joseph's public life if there hadn't been struggle and surrender in his private life. He had total confidence that God was working *"all things together for good."* His faith was rewarded when he was promoted to world-wide power and influence and when his family was blessed and saved. The fulfillment of God's work and plan was not only for his good, but it was a testimony to the world of God's goodness.

THE SECOND EXAMPLE
A BROKEN-HEARTED MOTHER

I am well acquainted with "The example of the Broken-Hearted Mother." You see, I experienced some of her pain and watched her as she faced overwhelming difficulties. The example of this little old widow was my mother's.

MY MOTHER WAS "GREATLY AFFLICTED"

As she sat in the funeral home listening to the minister eulogize her dead husband, there was not only pain in her aching heart, but a stabbing pain in her recently broken collar bone and shoulder. Her mind raced back to one year to this very day when her heroic son, **Wayne,** was killed in an automobile accident. He had spent three years overseas in the U.S. Marine Corp during World War II, only to be killed in a car wreck when he returned home. Now, in the same funeral home, one year to the day, November 6th, she is listening to a minister as he tries to comfort her family.

MOTHER OBSERVED HER CHILDREN

My mother, Elise Wilkins' thoughts were upon her ten remaining children, as she looked out over her family and friends. She saw them all pressed together in the front of the room, which had been reserved for "the family" during the funeral services.

There was **Alfred,** her oldest, who had his own wife and family, and they lived in Oklahoma. Alfred was a good Christian man. Next to him was **Joe,** who seemed very uncomfortable in his body cast. He was a brave, courageous man who had been wounded in two different battles in the recent war. Her third surviving son, **Clinton,** had learned bad habits while serving in the service. Although a good son, he drank and ran around on the weekends. **Elise Faye,** her oldest of two daughters, was a good girl nearing adulthood. **Jim** lived in his own world, while **Jackie** loved to fight. **Sammy, Margarett, Johnnie** and baby Charlie (age seven) were all good kids, **but none of them were saved or attended church.**

The services dragged on and in spite of the ministers words, there was nothing, humanly speaking, in which she could find comfort and hope.

OH LORD, WHAT AM I GOING TO DO?

Mother only had an eighth grade education and was in poor health. She had seen **dark days before, but nothing like this.** In her heart she kept crying, "Oh Lord, what am I going to do?" Thinking about the uncertain future, she could not see anything but the possibility of poverty, kids fussing and fighting, **problems** with school officials, **problems** with the law, **problems** paying the bills and **problems** just keeping the family together. Yes, the way seemed truly dark to her. **Truly dark!**

GOD HAS A SPECIAL PROVISION FOR SINGLE PARENTS

There are many places in the Scripture where God speaks of His love and care for the **fatherless and widows.** He makes a way and gives special provisions to those helpless women who rely upon Him.

81

OH LORD, THIS WILL I DO

Lord, I will devote myself entirely to You and in the raising of my children. **"Tempted and tired, we're oft made to wonder why it should be all the day long."** This is part of the words of an old hymn that I remember my mother singing. She sang this song in **a minor key,** which showed the hurt and loneliness she was experiencing as she continued to sing, **"farther along, we will understand why."**

That darkest of nights **began to turn to day,** as Elise, along with all of her younger children were in church **every time** the doors were opened. There was no quarreling and there was no fussing and fighting as God began to bless **that little old widow woman's prayers and faith.**

I WAS THE FIRST ONE SAVED

I, Jim Wilkins, was born the middle child in a family of **eleven** children and on July 10, 1949, experienced the joy that David describes in Psalm 116, as I too accepted Christ and was saved. This was quickly followed over the next five years, until everyone of the remaining ten children became devoted, practicing Christians.

FIVE PREACHER SONS

From the ten children, came five "fundamental" preachers, who worked to win souls, whether from the pulpit or from house to house. Others became faithful teachers, singers and servants of God in local churches. None were ever expelled from school and all were happily married – three of the oldest have celebrated "Golden Wedding Anniversaries" at the writing of this book.

MANY YEARS OF SUNSHINE AND JOY

Elise May Wilkins passed safely through her dark night of testing and lived many years surrounded by her children, grandchildren and relatives, who loved her as if she was their own mother. She enjoyed many years of sunshine and joy. Her constant message was, "God does not love one widow woman (single parent), more than He does another. Since He delivered me, then take courage, He will deliver you also."

PRAISE YE THE LORD!

Elise Wilkins, my mother, joined David as he walked down the **"Road to Victory."** She went home to join her husband and son with the assurance that **all eleven children** would soon join them. On her dying lips as she left this world, was David's theme song, **"Praise Ye the Lord!"**

THE THIRD EXAMPLE
THE VETERAN MISSIONARY

*O*ur third example, is that of a deserted preacher who wanted to die. His name and ministry is famous; and after all the sufferings he experienced, the problem, pain or situation **must have been indescribable.** Can you image anything **so bad that the great Apostle Paul wanted to die?**

I WANTED TO DIE

"I Was Greatly Afflicted" (Psalm 116:10). This statement could have been made by Paul in II Corinthians 1:8, when Paul spoke about his trouble in Asia he said,

- *"We were pressed out of measure,"*
- *"Above strength"* (I couldn't stand it),
- *"We despaired even of life"* (I wanted to die).

HOW BAD WAS BAD?

The Bible does not reveal what this particular tragedy in Paul's life was. He had health problems, was beaten three times with the whip (39 lashes each time), beaten with rods, shipwrecked, stoned, imprisoned with iron chains and left for dead. Plus he had numerous other mental and physical abuses. Whatever this experience was, it must have been indescribable for Paul to yearn and desire death.

THEN A STRANGE THING HAPPENED! He referred to this experience in order to explain the **joy and rejoicing,** which is recorded in II Corinthians 1:3-7. As Paul went through this horrible experience, which almost killed him, he even wanted to die; but now he rejoices and praises God for that experience.

Why? Oh, why does Paul now rejoice over such a heart-breaking experience?

It taught Paul how to comfort and "be there" for other people who would not have made it without him and the LESSONS he learned through his near death experience. Paul writes, *"Blessed be God, even the Father of our Lord Jesus Christ, the Father of mercies, and **the God of all comfort;** Who comforteth us in all our tribulation* (WHY?) ***that we may be able to comfort them,*** *which are in any trouble, by the comfort wherewith we ourselves are comforted of God"* (vv 3-4). Who? Comfort Who? Help Who? **Those we love the most** and others that God brings into our lives that desperately need someone who understands by experience their hurts and sorrow.

His Problems Helped Him "To Be There"

A PLAIN ENGLISH EXPLANATION! A person has a bad experience, "greatly afflicted." It comes out of the blue without warning. He, by the grace of God lives through it. Years later, He is able to help his children or others through similar experience, which SAVES THEIR LIVES and heals their hurts. Then, he understands WHY he had the bad experience, which as it turns out, was not a bad experience at all; it was GOD PREPARING **and** TEACHING him to "be there" to help save others.

A Dear Friend's Testimony

An old friend of mine told me that his bout with cancer, a tragic accident, three heart attacks and the death of his mother, prepared him for a ministry **to hurting people.** He would never have had this ability to minister without **his sufferings.** Having suffered himself, he can now empathize with those who are hurting and give them proper support.

THE FOURTH EXAMPLE
THE GOD OF ALL GRACE

*T*he Apostle Peter, writing to pastors in I Peter 5:10, made the following statement, *"But the*

God of all grace, who hath called us unto his eternal glory by Christ Jesus."

Notice the expression, *"the God of all Grace."* How much grace is "all Grace?" He provided grace for:

- Daniel in the lion's den,
- Paul and Silas in jail,
- Moses and the children of Israel facing the Red Sea, and
- Mary and Martha at their brother Lazarus' grave side,
- My mother during her darkest day, and
- My old friend through disease and heartbreak.

He promised grace **in every situation, in every generation** and **for every man** since the first man, Adam. He has enough grace and help to get you through each and every one of your problems, **if you will accept it.** He has helped and given grace to people who have gone through the exact trial **in which you are experiencing now!** The Bible tells us that the things we suffer are common to man and God will bring us through them.

HE IS THE GOD OF ALL GRACE!

He has a plan for you which is **for your eternal glory.** He will safely sustain you through any suffering, any task and any dark night, **if you will only trust Him and let Him.**

When you get through the experience,

- it will make you perfect (mature),
- it will establish you (as a Christian),
- it will strengthen you (with greater poise and confidence),
- and it will settle you (with more faith and hope).

"The God of all Grace, who hath called us unto his eternal glory by Christ Jesus, after that ye have suffered a while, make you perfect, stablish, strengthen, settle you" (I Peter 5:10).

God will use **the trials and afflictions,** in your life to teach you how **to overcome** and be a champion. Every dark night is always followed by the brilliant sunrise. You may not see the sun, but it is there. You may not be able to **see the Son, but He is there,** because He promised *"never to leave nor forsake you."*

Remember, we are in the world, but we are not of this world. Those of the world let troubles drive them to drink, drugs, insanity, divorce, depression and suicide. Troubles draw believers into the heart of God for help and healing. We are pilgrims and strangers on our way **home** (to heaven). We have the victory! The battle has been won, so let us lift up our heads and become champions. JOIN WITH THE OTHERS ALREADY ON THE **"ROAD TO VICTORY!"**

POINTS TO PONDER

- God safely took a young man (Joseph) through the school of heartbreak and loneliness and promoted him to rule the greatest nation on earth.

- God safely cared for an old widow and delivered her family to a life of happiness and service.

- God safely raised up an old preacher who was in such straits that he wanted to die, to the heights of a victorious life of joy and fruitfulness.

- God is the God of all Grace.

- God has a plan for your life.

- God will safely lift you up from any heartbreak, trouble or despair, which you may be enduring, because…

- God loves you!

- God is not a respecter of persons.

Lesson for Chapter Five

MONDAY
(Who Where Triumphant)

1. David was the _____ God chose to teach us how to live _____ heartbreak and became victorious.

2. Joseph starts life as a happy kid with _____ insight, who love to _____ about God.

3. One of his brothers, Judah, convinced the _____ to _____ him into slavery instead of killing him.

4. How frightened and horrified this _____ seventeen year old must have been as his _____ brothers heartlessly turned a deaf ear to his _____.

5. Joseph could have _____ the same statement that David did, *"all _____ are liars."*

TUESDAY
(The Training Period)

1. God put _____ in a carefully _____ school for the first 30 years of his life.

2. The way God chose to keep them from _____ to death was to _____ a seventeen year old boy.

3. Joseph reassured his _____, *"It was not you that sent me hither, but _____."*

4. Joseph's victory took place when he _____ God and _____ to self.

5. There would never have _____ the great _____ and _____ in Joseph's public life, if there hadn't been a _____ in his private life.

WEDNESDAY
(A BROKEN-HEARTED MOTHER)

1. There was nothing, _____ speaking, in which she could find _____ and hope.

2. He makes a way and _____ special provisions to those helpless _____ who rely upon Him.

3. Lord, I will devote myself _____ to you and in raising my _____.

4. That darkest of _____ began to turn to _____.

5. On her dying _____, as she left this
   _____, was _____ theme song.

THURSDAY
(THE VETERAN MISSIONARY)

1. Can you imagine anything so _____ that the
   great Apostle _____ wanted to die?
2. He referred to this _____ in order to
   _____ the _____ and rejoicing.
3. It taught him how to _____ and "be
   _____" for other people.
4. Who? Comfort _____? Help _____?
   Those we _____ the most.
5. It was God _____ and _____ him to
   "be there" to help others.

FRIDAY
(THE GOD OF ALL GRACE)

1. How much _____ is "_____ Grace?"

2. He promised _____ in every _____, in
   every _____, and for _____ man.

3. He will safely sustain you through any
   _____, any task and any dark night, if you
   will only _____ Him and let Him.

4. God will use the _____ and _____, in
   your _____ to teach you how to overcome
   and be a champion.

5. You may not be able to see the _____, but He
   is there, because He _____ *"never to leave
   nor forsake you."*

COMMITMENT TO EXCELLENCE

Having learned how God helped the young, the old,
and the preacher and that He is the God of all grace, I
will strive daily to know His will and direction for my
life through prayer and Bible study. In order to be
triumphant, I must live in the grace of God, so I now
surrender my problems and life to Him.

_____   _____

Name   Date

DAILY FAITH BUILDER

CHAPTER FIVE

DAILY DECLARATION:

God, if you loved and helped the others, you will surely help me. **Repeat this phrase aloud each morning and evening.**

MEMORY VERSE:

"For there is no difference between the Jew and the Greek: for the same Lord over all is rich unto all that call upon him" (Romans 10:12).

CHECK BLOCK AFTER REPEATING

Mon	Tues	Wed	Thurs	Fri	Sat	Sun
A.M.						
P.M.						

Grade: _____

E-MAILS TO GOD

E-MAILS From a World Leader:

Dear God,

> *Why don't you stop all the wars in the world?*

Dear World Leader,

> *I didn't start them. God*

E-MAIL From a Puzzled Parent:

Dear God,

> *Why don't you stop all the high school shootings?*

Dear Puzzled Parent,

> *Remember, I am not allowed in schools anymore. God*

E-MAIL From a Single Parent:

Dear God,

> *Why did you let my marriage break-up?*

Dear Single Parent,

> *I gave you a manual for preserving your marriage, but you did not read it. God*

E-MAIL From a Troubled Soul:

Dear God,

> *I've got a problem! Help!*

Dear Troubled Soul,

> *I've been waiting for you to call. Let's get together. I want to help! God*

Chapter Six

CHAPTER SIX

TWO EXERCISES FOR
HEALING AND HAPPINESS

*J*n Chapter One, the author attempted to give the scriptural foundation using Psalm 116, which instructs a person in how to deal with offenses. However, even though the Scriptures were clearly presented, the author realized that those seeking help needed to know how to apply them to their lives, personally.

Chapters Two and Three show the three major reactions to offenses and heartbreak, as well as the results of each reaction. Again, this knowledge is important, but a hurting person needs more direction than just determination of a particular category which he may fit into.

Chapter Four explains why human beings have problems and how God works to help us during our struggles. Although Chapter Four revealed why the human race has problems, it gave no practical help in solving these problems.

In Chapter Five, we show the triumphance of those who availed themselves of God's grace during their trials and God's willingness to help any man, under any circumstances. Although this is reassuring and gives hope to a hurting person, it does not give him the specific steps to take, in order to find peace and happiness.

In this final chapter, we will share two practical exercises, which the wounded must perform in order to be whole again.

The first principle is developed under the heading of *"Let the dead bury the dead."* The second principle is the exercise one must learn to do in order to **forgive one's self.**

YOU ARE IMPORTANT TO GOD!

*I*t **doesn't matter** what you have said about God. **It doesn't matter** that you are angry toward God. **It doesn't matter** how you have sinned or what sin you are involved in right now! **It doesn't matter** how many people you have disappointed or hurt. That is all in the past; you are alive now and God wants to help you obtain the best life you can have for the rest of your life. This has always been His goal for you and **He hasn't changed His mind about YOU!**

WHAT MATTERS NOW IS THAT GOD LOVES YOU!

He is touched by your feelings and your pain! He has compassion toward you and longs to help you. **WHAT MATTERS TO GOD IS WHAT YOU DECIDE TO DO NOW!**

"I QUIT!" REALLY?

*H*ow long ago was it when you suffered your heartbreak? Who was it that wounded you?

Instead, let me ask, "What was it that wounded you?" It probably pains you to think about it. You may have tried to bury it, seal it off, or program yourself to not think about it. Maybe the problem is that you think about your heartbreak **too much!** Whatever you are doing, wouldn't you like to be free of it?

YOUR REAL PROBLEM

You "QUIT," in that you stopped going to church. But you still have the problem. That horrible experience still rules your life.

It changed you!

It robbed you!

It is still robbing you!

WOULDN'T YOU LIKE TO BE FREE?

Wouldn't you like to take a deep breath and just push it out of your system, like **exhaling the air** from your lungs? **Wouldn't you like to be free? You can be!**

WHAT MORE CAN I DO BUT SAY, "I'M SORRY"

*T*here isn't much more that I can do than to say, "I'm sorry." During the past 50 years in my ministry, **I have been hurt, seen hurt, lived through hurt** and **I truly know how you are hurting.** I am sorry for your wounds and sorrow, and though my sympathy may help a little, that is all it can do – just help a little.

I can point out some principles and the horrible end results of quitting church and how it hinders the purpose of God for your life. I can point out what happens when you become bitter and **spew that bitterness** out on your children, loved ones and friends.

But I cannot:

**HEAL THE PAIN,
HEAL YOUR HEART,
OR
RESTORE YOUR JOY.**

TWO HEALING EXERCISES

*T*here are two final principles (actions) which the wounded person must undertake in order to find peace and victory. The first, is to put your priorities in order and *"let the dead bury the dead."* In other words, concentrate on the needs of the living. The second principle, is the exercise of learning and acting to forgive yourself.

1. *"LET THE DEAD BURY THE DEAD."*

This is what Jesus told a grieving disciple one day when that disciple asked Jesus to let him bury his father FIRST before following Him. *"Follow me; and let the dead bury their dead"* (Matthew 8:22), was the command Jesus gave to the inquiring disciple.

YOU CANNOT HELP THE DEAD

He died! He could no longer hear anyone. You cannot go back to the past when the dead were still living. **He is gone** – dead – beyond our ability to reach. In other words, Jesus told the disciple to let him go!

Let the dead bury the dead, also refers to **dead issues.** Please stop resurrecting dead issues which haunt you. Bury the ghosts of the past with all their haunting memories. Give them up, put them in the past, and do as Jesus said, *"Come follow me."*

JESUS HELPS THE LIVING

So many people lament over the bad things of the past, that they do not think, love, or care for those **who are alive** and who need their love, comfort and encouragement in the present.

CRIPPLED BY THE PAST

By being consumed by the heartbreak, the wound, the bad deal (the "greatly afflicted" experience), they become crippled and **held captive by the past.** Their thoughts are inward: dwelling upon themselves. The hurts IN THEIR PAST are alive; that is, they still exist in their minds, but in reality, they are letting themselves be held captive to the things of the past **which are dead!** You have to get **past the past** in order **to ever have a future!**

JESUS SAID THAT YOU CAN BE FREE!

"How?" you may ask.

"By following the command of Jesus," I would answer.

Jesus said, *"Let the dead* (the past = the things you cannot change) *bury the dead, and come and follow me."*

WHAT DOES IT MEAN,
"*LET THE DEAD BURY THE DEAD?*"

It means, let it go – concentrate on the living (the present). Leave the problem in the past! It's over, you cannot do anything to change what happened. Let it go – it's buried!

THE HEALING COMES

When you leave the past, bury it and start following Jesus in helping the living: those who need you, who love you, who are going to PERISH unless you minister to them. Then, and only then, are you going to get over the bad decision which you made when you QUIT.

JESUS IS WAITING!

He still loves you! He misses your love and fellowship **so much**. He has been **waiting on you** to ask Him for help – He has wanted to heal you – FOR SO LONG! **Read this little paragraph three or four times.** You may even have a loved one that needs to hear it – today!

ALL IT TAKES

He is God! He is your Creator! He is the Great Physician. Jesus once asked a crippled man, "*Will thou be made whole?*" The man had been looking all his life to the wrong source for his healing. *"The impotent man answered him, Sir, I have no man,"* (John 5:6-7). Then the crippled man made the wisest decision of his life. He looked to Jesus, and Jesus as God, healed him and made him whole.

All it takes for you to find peace and be healed of your wound, is for you to look to Jesus. Ask Jesus to help you and He will cleanse and make you whole again. When that happens, you will be able to forgive the person who hurt you.

This will enable you to bury the past. When you bury the past and begin to follow Jesus, **you will be free.**

When you are free, you will better realize how to help your loved ones and others. When you begin to help the living, you will have the joy and peace that you never expected to have again.

Why don't you bow your head and **begin that process right now?**

2. THE EXERCISE OF FORGIVING ONE'S SELF

This final principle that many of the wounded must learn and do, is to **forgive themselves.** Master the following exercise and you will be free from past guilt!

DEALING WITH PAST GUILT

*S*ince more people develop guilt and bitterness from the loss of a dear loved one through death than any other reason, we will use **guilt and bitterness that develops from death** to demonstrate how to deal with guilt and bitterness, **regardless of its origin.**

Immediately after the death of a loved one, comes a flood of questions. Among those questions are some with very sharp edges. These edges hurt, they accuse and they bring assertions which make one cry and feel guilty. Most of these thoughts come due to the normal process of bereavement after the death of a loved one. There are times, however, when there has been a breakdown in the relationship: a differences of opinion, **misdeeds, or harsh words,** which cause regret and guilt. This guilt could present a real problem, which could affect a person adversely for the rest of his life. It may wound or destroy many others if it is not dealt with properly.

1. DEAL IN REALITY

Let us attempt to think through this real problem and guide you from guilt, back to a higher and a more productive plane of living.

Let us think realistically. You are an **imperfect person** and are capable of **making mistakes** and **doing wrong.**

Your loved one was also an **imperfect person** and was capable of **making mistakes** and **doing wrong.**

We live in an **imperfect world,** which contributes to our distractions and **failures.** Many times, we intend to do things and do not get them done. We **carelessly let things slide** without any thought or intent of **harm.** Many times, this unintentional delay is the very thing that **causes the problem** or at least **makes the problem worse.**

2. THERE WERE GOOD TIMES

Remember all the good times that you and your loved one or friend had together.

Go over those good times in your mind. It may be painful, but you must think about it. **Do not** just remember your mistakes or the specific thing(s) that caused you to feel guilty. **Go back before** the problem(s) or offense(s) occurred.

Think! Remember! There were some good times and pleasant memories. Remember them. Most of the time, **you responded properly; especially** when you were really needed or the person was counting on you. **Dwell on those good times.** Think about all of the **pleasant experiences.**

3. THINK OF THE TIMES WHEN YOU "CAME THROUGH"

Think of all the help and the good that you gave that person. Again, make yourself think of the favors you did him. Often times, we don't realize how much support we do give our friends. Think back on the times he needed you, and how you supported him. Go back beyond the past few days or months. How many times did you "come through" for that person during your relationship with him? Focus on **those** times.

4. WHAT DO YOU FEEL GUILTY ABOUT?

Think of the time or times you failed that person. Think of whatever you did or said that you **judged** to be wrong. Get those events clearly focused in your mind. It may hurt, but you can do it. Now, answer the following questions:

- **Would that person have understood** your frailty or lack of support at the time?

- **Would that person want you to keep punishing yourself** over this problem or offense? Is it benefiting you or anyone else for you to keep feeling the guilt you are feeling?

- **Would that person forgive you** if you asked him to do so? With all of the remorse and regret you are now feeling, if you were able to ask his forgiveness, would he forgive you?

- **Now, at this time,** stop reading and **ask him to forgive you!** Whatever it was, in whatever way you choose, call him by name and ask him for forgiveness. This is very important! Did you ask him? Okay! That's great! Now then, let's continue on with our cleansing experience.

- **Now, forgive yourself.** You are evidently sorry for the breakdown, the hurt, and the failure it has caused. It will not do any good to keep carrying the guilt around with you. Say to yourself, "Now, I am forgiving myself," and then continue on in the present by celebrating all of the good times you had together, instead of the bad.

- **Maybe you are the one who was slighted or was hurt and embittered and you are holding a grudge.** If you are, realize how insignificant the hurt was, and let it go. Tell God you are sorry for continuing in sin by not forgiving your friend or relative, and forgive him for hurting you. You will find a true peace in doing so.

5. LET THAT MISTAKE, MAKE YOU A BETTER PERSON

Remember, the ball game is not over until the final batter is out. The season is not over until the final game is played. The rest of your life is still ahead of you. Let the mistakes of your past make you into a wiser, more considerate person. You can do this in the following ways:

a. **Make up for past failures** by becoming **a more thoughtful person** in your daily life by considering the needs of others.

b. **Don't overdo it.** Be yourself as you accept your role in your family and in the outside world. Strive to let this bad experience **teach you,** so you can become **a more thoughtful, helpful person.**

c. **If the guilt returns to haunt you,** repeat to yourself "Yes, I did fail, but I forgive myself and now I am becoming a better person, **because of what I learned from that failure.**"

6. IF YOU CAN, MAKE IT RIGHT

If there is any restitution, then make it. If there is anything you can do for **another person** who may have been hurt, because of your action, then do it. Do your very best to correct your error. **If your honest effort is not accepted by the other person, do not let that keep you from confessing the wrong and then leaving it behind you in the past.** Concentrate on helping **the living** instead of **lamenting over the dead.** You are obligated to help the living. They need you, and you can help them. When you have done all that you can do to make restitution toward that loved one, **do not dwell on the failures,** but let it stimulate you to being a better person toward others.

a. **Repeat this thought process as often as necessary.** If you do need to repeat this process, do it until you discover how to allow the past to become a good teacher, which will elevate you to a happier, more fruitful level of life, at peace with the past.

THANK GOD FOR THE EXPERIENCE

I certainly do not mean that you thank God for **the offense(s) which caused your guilt.** What I do mean is, to **thank God for the growth** that you have experienced in overcoming the guilt. Thank Him for **the insight and understanding,** which now replaces the guilt that was destroying your life. If you had not had this sad experience where you failed or where you let someone you loved down, **you probably would have continued on in your life just as you were** and would probably make the same mistake again and again. Many people are so concerned about self and their own personal feelings that **they do not realize how their self-centeredness is affecting other people.**

Now, you can reach out and aid others who have similar problems. By **accepting** forgiveness from the deceased and by learning how to **forgive yourself,** you will have **matured** greatly as a person. What you should thank God for, is the liberty and peace that comes from your experience.

7. NOW VISUALIZE THE FOLLOWING:

Visualize writing down your wound on a piece of paper. Then visualize writing down your offense or guilt on the same piece of paper. Write down everything that is troubling you and causing you hurt or guilt regarding your lost loved one. Write it all down – the things you feel guilty about, the unforgiving spirit you have maintained, the grudge you have carried, the hurt over being misunderstood – put it all down on paper. Is there anything you have left off regarding yourself, others, God? Write it all down.

Now, go into the bathroom and tear the paper into little bits and flush the pieces down the commode. Watch them swirling around and around and then down they go, out of sight. As they disappear, tell yourself that as the pieces have been flushed away, you are flushing the thoughts that have been troubling you, from your life. They are now gone!

As you leave the bathroom, leave with the determination to join God and walk as David walked on his **"Road to Victory!"**

YOU HAVE DISCOVERED YOUR PROBLEM

*S*ome of you as you read these pages have discovered **your real problem – YOU** have never been born-again (saved). You are morally a good person and may even attend church services, but you do not really know Jesus in a personal way. Others who have read along have doubted THEIR standing with God for a long time.

NOW IS THE TIME

*N*ow, wherever you are sitting, it is time to settle these doubts and make sure you have a personal relationship with God.

First, think of the sins in your life and admit you are a sinner (Romans 3:23).

Second, realize according to God's Word, the Bible, that if you should die today, you would be separated from God in Hell forever.

Third, realize that God loves you and gave His Son, Jesus, to die on the cross and has already paid for your sins (Romans 5:8).

Fourth, God has promised that anyone who understands that he is separated from Him by his sins and who will ask Him to accept the death of Jesus as payment for his sins, will be forgiven (Romans 10:13).

Fifth, now bow your head and honestly repeat this prayer:

Dear God,

> *I know that I am a sinner. Please forgive me of my sins and save me from Hell.*
>
> *Jesus, please come into my heart. I now accept you as my Savior, and from this day on, I will live for you.*
>
> *In Jesus' Name, Amen*

Jesus made this promise,

"If the Son therefore shall make you free, YE SHALL BE FREE INDEED" (John 8:36).

Again, the Bible promises whosoever (you) shall call upon the name of the Lord shall be saved (from hell) (Romans 10:13).

Now, you are truly free! Obey the command of Jesus, *"Follow me"* (Matthew 8:22), and you will be freed from the past.

Look to Jesus for your daily needs and you will have a bright future! You will become one of the hurting masses who met the Healer and was made whole!

You Can Be Like David

When David died to self, he wanted to share his victorious story with everyone. God raised him up and made him a great blessing to his generation. Your generation needs someone to love and help them. Let God make you a David to your family and friends... Remember, David's theme song was **"Praise Ye The Lord!"**

FROM THE AUTHOR

The Back to Basics Follow-up, Protection and Development and Rehabilitation Program is based upon the teachings found in the pastoral commission as given to Peter by Jesus in John 21:15-17. Jesus very emphatically spelled out Peter's responsibility as pastor in three separate charges.

1. *"Feed my Lambs,"* or literally stated, "pacify my babies."
2. *"Feed my Sheep,"* the ones who are weak, sick or lame.
3. *"Feed my Sheep,"* the strong, healthy, prime, fruitful sheep.

These charges to the first pastor teach the **methodology of feeding** as well as the **responsibility for feeding**. It also teaches the way an infant learns – by observing the example set before him.

The pastor, as tender nurse (I Thessalonians 2:7) or Spiritual Father (I Thessalonians 2:11), sets the proper role-model before God's family and trains the members of the Church by his example (**holy, just and blameless** [I Thessalonians 2:10] and **exhorting, comforting and charging** [I Thessalonians 2:11]), until they have made the transition from defenseless babes to fully grown, working saints.

He trains the older members of his church to become role-models: (pastor's assistants) taking the milk of the Word to the new converts and **pacifying** (loving, protecting and giving them security) them until they are able to walk alone and are secure in the church family.

NEW CONVERTS CARE DISCIPLESHIP PROGRAM

The Follow-Up Phase: As soon as a person is born-again he needs to have the shield of faith put on him. This is done by giving him a new birth certificate and teaching him seven principles that will protect and help him to grow (found in the Salvation to Service booklet).

Salvation to Service Booklet

Questions Concerning Baptism

Four Transformational Truths (4 week study)

The Protection and Development Phase: A spiritual role-model is appointed over the new convert as an extension of the pastor's ministry for three to six months. By living in a just and unblamable way, the role-model sets a good example for the new convert. He also goes through the Milk of the Word with the new convert, helping him learn how to rightly divide the Word (in other words, feed himself) until he can study alone.

Milk of the Word (10 week study)
Mission of the Church (12 week study)
Meat of the Word (10 week study)

The Rehabilitation Phase The statement Jesus made to the first pastor, *"Feed My Sheep"* (wounded and hurting), teaches that there is a need in many Christian lives for rehabilitation. Something in their lives has completely stopped them from growing, or is **restricting their spiritual growth in some way.** They have been wounded or offended and have retreated within themselves. They desperately need the information found in these lessons, loving encouragement and rehabilitation.

Helping Hands for Hurting People (4 week study)

BOOKS FOR SOUL-WINNING TRAINING

Essentials for Successful Soul-Winning
Foreknowledge in the Light of Soul-Winning
Designed to Win

Churches: Please contact **New Testament Ministries** for quantity prices.

For a complete listing of the author's books,
E-mail www.pWilkins96@ sbcglobal.com
Our website address is www.jameswilkins.org

New Testament Ministries
Dr. James Wilkins, Director
P.O. Box 291
Bedford, TX 76095
(817) 267-6239